GRASSES

by

Irmengarde Eberle

illustrated by

Ezra Jacks Keats

NEW YORK   HENRY Z. WALCK, INCORPORATED   1960

To Linda Novak

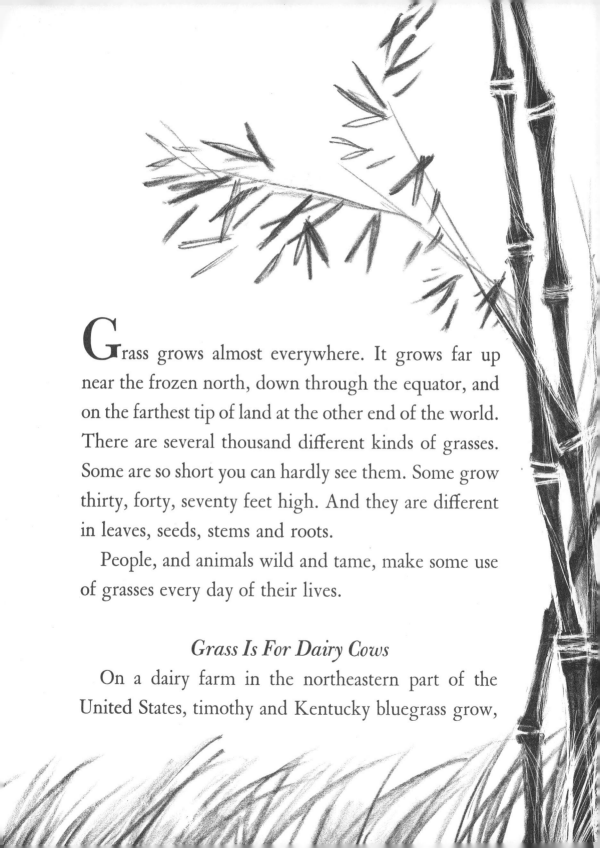

Grass grows almost everywhere. It grows far up near the frozen north, down through the equator, and on the farthest tip of land at the other end of the world. There are several thousand different kinds of grasses. Some are so short you can hardly see them. Some grow thirty, forty, seventy feet high. And they are different in leaves, seeds, stems and roots.

People, and animals wild and tame, make some use of grasses every day of their lives.

Grass Is For Dairy Cows

On a dairy farm in the northeastern part of the United States, timothy and Kentucky bluegrass grow, and scattered patches of other grasses. In the spring and summer when the grass is greenest the dairy farmer keeps his cows in the meadows and feeds them little else. And the milk they give then is particularly rich and good.

When he milks his cows, mornings and evenings, he uses electric milking machines. All big dairy farms have them now. If he has only a few cows he milks by hand. He leaves plenty of milk for the young calves, enough for his family, and has big canfuls to sell. He sets the cans by the roadside for the tank truck to pick up. It takes them to a plant that buys milk from many farmers.

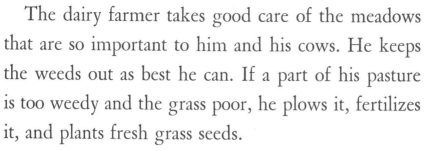

The dairy farmer takes good care of the meadows that are so important to him and his cows. He keeps the weeds out as best he can. If a part of his pasture is too weedy and the grass poor, he plows it, fertilizes it, and plants fresh grass seeds.

On well-cared-for acres the grass will grow strong and dense. Its thick tangle of leaves and roots stops

many of the weed seeds that drift in from finding a place to take root and spread.

There are many kinds of pasture grasses—twenty-four or so in the northeastern states alone.

In the summer the cows stay outdoors all the time except during milking hours. In the winter when there is ice and snow on the ground the farmer keeps his valuable dairy cows in their stalls in the big barn much of the time. There he feeds them hay and a mixture made up largely of cracked, flaked or crushed dry grains such as oats, corn, barley and sometimes wheat. Both hay and grain come from grasses. And from his tall silo near the barn the farmer brings the cows juicy silage, which is largely chopped-up, green, young corn —also a grass. Almost everything he feeds his cows the year round is grass food—leaves, stems and seeds.

For Ranch Cattle and Horses

The grasses of the western prairies are food for great herds of beef cattle and cattlemen's horses. The cattle graze under the open sky far from ranch houses or towns the year round. Blue grama grass, buffalo grass, switch grass and others grow on the western prairies.

On the ranch too the owner has to watch his grass. He and his men often ride out to the places where the cattle graze. If the cattle stay very long in one place they nibble the grass too close to the ground, and trample the earth down hard, so that the grass can't grow up from the roots again. This is called over-grazing.

A good rancher doesn't let it happen. He and his cowboys drive the herd away to another part of the range from time to time. Then none of the grass on the ranch is killed by overgrazing.

Ranchers, like dairy farmers, sometimes plant grass on parts of their pastures. They want to make still better grazing grounds. And often they plant grasses that stay green into the cold weather.

Though many ranch horses are put into stables in bad weather, the great herds of ranch cattle have no home but the open range. There are too many of them to put in barns.

Once in a while a drought comes and dries the grass, and no new shoots come up. Then the range cattle can't find anything to eat. The rancher feeds them hay,

but they need grass too. If the drought goes on for
long he drives or ships his cattle to good grasslands
in other parts of the country.

Blizzards are hard on the cattle. These fierce winter storms don't come very often to the cattle-ranch states. But when they do, the snow covers the ground deeply. The cattle can't get at the sparse winter grass at all. Starving and freezing in the bitter cold, many of them die.

The rancher must do something quickly to save the rest of his cattle. He buys a lot of hay from a feed dealer, and he and his men load it on trucks and take it out to the cattle.

But sometimes the snow is too deep, and the trucks can't get through the drifts. Then the rancher may rent an airplane. He loads it with hay and cuts the wires of the bales. The pilot flies the load out to the range. Skimming low over the prairie he drops the opened bales down to the hungry cattle. So they stay alive in the snow with the help of the dry grass, hay.

For Goats

In summertime the farmers of Switzerland graze their milk goats and cows on the steep slopes and valleys of their mountain country. The cows graze on the lower slopes, the goats on the high rocky ones. Alpine grasses called wavy mountain hair grass, and Alpen Rispen, and a kind of wild oats, grow richly green after the snow has melted.

In the first warm days of the year the goat herders take their animals up the mountains. Sure-footed, the goats climb the rocks and find between them the juicy grass they love. The men or boys follow to see that no harm comes to them. Sometimes a goat gets out on a small ledge above a cliff and can't get back. The herder sees him and calls for help, and another man watching his animals on a nearby slope comes running. One man then lowers the other on a rope till he reaches the ledge. He picks up the goat, and man and animal are pulled up to safety.

Many of the herders have huts in the mountains. They live there alone, or with their families, and watch their grazing goats and care for them. They milk them and make wonderful cheeses of the milk.

The chill of autumn comes early to these high places. Then the herder brings his goats and his cheeses down to the home farm in the valley. When the cheeses are properly aged and ripened he sells them.

The farming people of Switzerland are dependent on the grass of their country. It feeds the animals by which they make their living.

For Llamas

Llamas graze on the high slopes of the Andes Mountains of South America. Ichu and festuca are some of the most common grasses there. The Peruvians have tamed llamas and used them as work animals for many centuries. There are wild llamas, called guanacos, running free among the peaks and crags.

Llamas are better than horses or donkeys for work
high in the mountains, for they can breathe comfort-
ably and carry heavy loads at heights of twelve to six-
teen thousand feet. Most animals are weakened by lack
of oxygen in the air in these places, and can't work.
But the llamas can carry loads of two hundred pounds
trotting fifteen miles a day. They are used for bring-
ing ore out of the mines among the rocky upper peaks.
Great droves of llamas, sometimes as many as several
hundred or a thousand, come along the narrow roads
in long lines carrying the ore.

Farmers who cultivate little patches of land in the mountains use llamas too. They load their farm products on the animals' backs and bring them down to the towns where they can be sold in the markets.

Some llamas are all white, others are spotted brown and white, others are a dark brown. In the summer they feed on grasses and leaves of shrubbery. The farmers cut tall meadow grasses and keep them, so that they can feed the llamas in cold weather when there isn't much fresh grass. Then the tame llamas don't have to rove far in search of grass, as the wild guanacos do.

Hay Farming

All the grazing animals people raise—horses, sheep, dairy cows, beef cattle, llamas, goats—need hay some time of the year. So, in many countries, farmers grow hay as an important crop. And hay is just meadow grass grown tall and cut and dried in the sun. But some kinds of grass make better hay than others, and farmers cultivate these.

Some people grow just enough hay for their own farm animals. They store it either loose or in bales in their barns until they need it. And if at haying time they have more than will go into the barns, they make haystacks or hayricks nearby.

Some farmers, particularly the large hay farmers of the United States, grow nothing else on their land. And they sell hundreds of bales to companies that market the hay.

Such a farmer has many acres of good, level land. He may have wild meadow grass that makes fine hay growing in some of his fields. But he has to plant many acres of grass from seed, too.

The farmer lets the grass grow tall. But he does not wait until seeds form on it, for he does not want any of the strength of the plants to go into these. He is growing the grass only for the food in its leaves and stems. Nor does he wait till the leaves of the grass turn yellow and dry. He cuts his hay while it is still fresh and juicy.

The harvesting begins in the latter part of the summer or in early autumn. The farmer attaches a hay cutter to his tractor, with a blade five or more feet long. With it he drives through the field and cuts down the hay. He lets it lie there to dry in the sun-

shine. But it is only the water that dries out. The food values stay in the leaves and stems.

When the hay is dry enough to store, the farmer and his helpers bring out the baler. A baling machine is costly, and so several farmers of a region sometimes buy one together and take turns using it. But large hay farmers who grow no other crops usually have one of their own.

As the machine is driven through the field it picks up bunches of the dry grass, presses them into bales, ties them with wire and drops them to the ground. A baler can make round rolls of hay with one attachment and the regular rectangular ones with another.

The hay farmer sells his bales to companies that deal in cattle feed. These in turn sell to dairy farmers, ranchers, and people who have riding horses, donkeys or mules.

Corn

Many grasses bear grain that is an important food for people as well as animals. Corn is one of these. When the first settlers came to America, they found that the Indians ate corn. Corn has been much changed since then, and many different kinds have been developed. People eat corn muffins, corn flakes, and, perhaps best of all, fresh young green corn boiled, buttered and salted.

Special varieties of corn are grown for all the different uses. The farmer gives whole, crushed, flaked or cracked feed corn to his pigs and chickens and cattle. The entire corn plants, while still green, are used in silage. Silage, which is made in a round, tall vatlike building that stands near the barn, has several other things in it. Green hay is sometimes added, and plants like alfalfa, which are not grass, and sometimes molasses. Molasses comes from a grass plant too—sugar cane.

Early in the summer the farmer plows and fertilizes his cornfields. He cuts into the earth with the plow, making furrows about eighteen inches apart. When the field is ready he puts his seed corn into a long, narrow box on wheels which he then fastens to the tractor.

This is the seed drill. The box has movable pipes, and as he drives along the furrows the pipes are lowered, and each sets several seeds well down into the earth. Eighteen to twenty inches farther on it sets more seeds into the ground. They are spaced far apart like this so that the plants won't crowd each other as they grow.

When the corn is several feet high it is sprayed from a tank on a truck, to protect it against insects. Or, if the fields are very big, a small airplane is sometimes used.

If a farmer has planted the kind of corn that people

eat fresh, he picks the ears while the kernels are still young and tender and full of sweet, milky juice.

Feed corn is harvested in the late summer or early autumn. The stalks and their long, ribbonlike leaves have wilted and dried by that time and are a light yellow-brown. The corn ears which grow close to the stalk have become dry too, and the kernels are hard.

Corn that is to be ground into meal has to be dry too before it is sent to the mill.

Now the farmer takes men into the field to help him pick the dry ears. Or he brings out another modern machine—the corn picker. When he works with the corn picker a helper drives a truck along beside him. Movable steel claws stick out from each side of the picker. When the farmer pushes a button these claws reach out, grab the ears, and shake their dry husks loose. Next they rip the ears out of their husks and off the corn stalks. They drop them onto a webbed belt which rolls them into the truck.

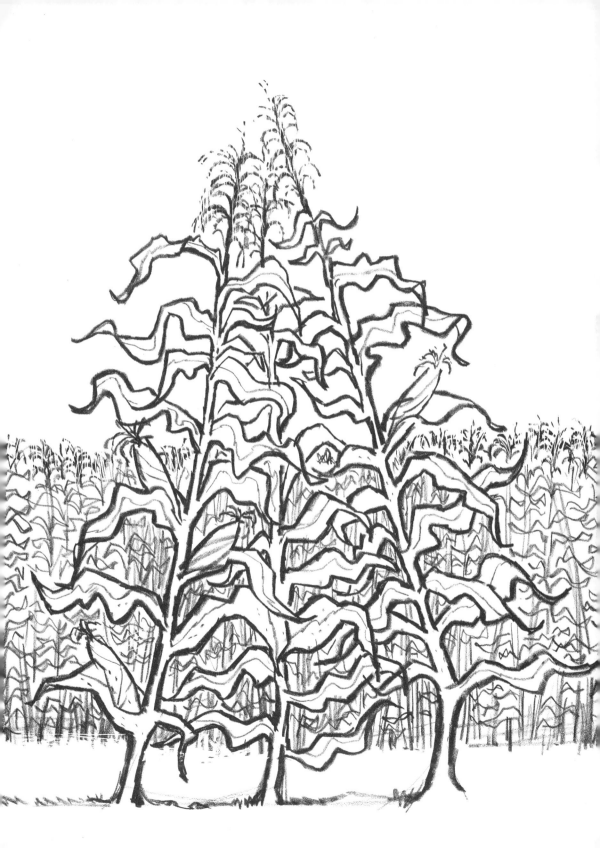

When the truck is full of corn its driver takes it off the field and dumps the load into a steel crib. There the dry corn is stored. The farmer sells it when he can get a good price. Or, if he has grown the corn only for his own use, he stores it as feed for his pigs, chickens and turkeys.

The dry corn kernels have to be rubbed off the cobs before they can be used. And this too is mostly done by a machine on the farm, or at a mill.

Wheat

Wheat has been, for many centuries, the most important grain of Europe. It was used there for ages before American corn became known. It is made into millions of loaves of bread and millions of cakes in America and abroad every day.

Wheat is not planted in rows like corn. Its seeds are scattered over the field. At first when the plants begin to grow green and tall they look much like young hay. But soon the seed heads form. Each is made up of dozens of small, plump seeds covered with crisp husks. Thin spikes stick out at the top, giving the heads a lacy look.

Wheat ripens at various times through the summer, for there are different kinds, and some are planted earlier than others. Toward autumn the grass stalks and grain heads turn yellow-brown and dry. The wheat must be harvested before the seeds fall off.

American farmers use a large machine called a combine. It may be rented, or it may be owned by a group of farmers. They move it from place to place as the different farmers need it. With it the farmer cuts down the standing wheat grass. The machine feeds it into itself and threshes it, separating the grain from the straw and the dry, crisp hulls from each seed. The wheat is weighed and put into the farmer's own gran-ary. Or the machine puts it into trucks so that the farmer can drive it away to sell. It is stored in the tall, narrow buildings called grain elevators, which stand beside the railroad tracks. In a grain elevator the grain can be hoisted up and poured out in a great stream into the railroad cars. These carry it to flour mills and feed companies.

Rice

In India, China, Japan, Burma, Malaya and other countries of the East, rice is the most important food. Though it originally came from there, it is now grown in other warm parts of the world, particularly in southern Europe and America. The rice plant too is a grass.

In the East, on a small farm, a whole family works together to plant rice. They first plant the grain in a wet seed bed. The seed begins to sprout, and small green shoots show above the soil. The shoots grow a little taller, not quite a foot high. Then the people transplant them into a field called a paddy.

Walking backward, they set the plants in rows on each side of them. When the whole field is planted, they pump water into it through a ditch they have dug from a nearby stream. A low mud wall all around the field holds the water in.

Rice grows well only when it is standing deep in water during most of the time of its growth. The tops of the grass are above water, and it is here that the grain heads form and slowly ripen. In from three to six months the plants turn a light yellow-brown. Then the family opens the mud walls around the field at several places and lets the water drain off.

They wait a few days until the earth and the plants have had time to dry out. Then they gather the grain by hand. They throw the stalks on hard, trampled ground and beat them with sticks or with a pole balanced somewhat like a seesaw. They gather up the rice that falls off and beat it again to get the dry hulls off. Next they pour it from baskets or other vessels and let the wind carry off the loosened hulls, or chaff. Then at last they have their rice—brown rice, and good food.

In modern countries where machinery is in use, rice growing is easier, and farmers usually do it on a larger scale. The seeds are planted with machines, and the harvesting and thrashing is done by large combines much like those used for wheat. Before it is put in packages, the brown color is taken off the grain in refineries, and the white rice is polished by the machines through which it is run.

Sugar Cane

Sugar cane is a tall grass that people grow for the sweet juice in its stems. It grows in hot, moist lands near the sea, and especially well on tropical islands like Hawaii and the West Indies. On these islands many of the plantations are very big. The fields are laid out in squared-off sections with roads running between them so that the men can go on foot or in trucks to do their work.

The men plant the cane from cuttings. Each cutting has a joint of the stem in it. These, when set in the ground, quickly put out roots in the wet earth. The hot sun shines on them, green sprouts rise upward, and

the new young crop starts growing. Full grown, the sugar cane stands several feet higher than a man's head. It is left to ripen for about two years, for the longer it stands the sweeter its juice is.

When it is ready to be harvested, the field workers come and cut it down. In some places this is still done by hand with big, heavy knives called machetes. In many other places it is cut by machines.

On some of the very big plantations tracks are laid through the fields, and trains bring the cane out. On other plantations trucks are used.

The men put chain nets in the bottom of their long, open trailer trucks before they fill them with cane. Later, when they have brought the load to the mill, hooks from overhead grab the chain nets and dump the whole load of cane onto a moving belt. The belt carries it into the mill where it is stripped of leaves by machinery and cut into pieces. Next it is shredded, and then crushed by great rollers so that the sweet juice runs out. This juice, cleaned of the cane leaves and stalks that float in it, is boiled down to a syrup. And finally, in great heated vats, the syrup is whirled around so that the sugar crystals separate from the water. These again are treated to make them white, and the white crystals are ground fine to make powdered or granulated sugar.

Changing the Grasses

Because so many grasses are important to people and their animals, men have changed and improved them. Some men run large farms only to develop better corn, wheat or pasture grass, sugar cane or other plants. They are plant breeders.

They change the plants by putting the dustlike flower pollen of one kind into the flower cups of another kind. In this way they get the good qualities of both in a new variety. The grasses are also improved by selecting the best seeds from the crop each year and planting them the next year. Or cuttings of the best stems may be taken to plant, as is done with sugar cane. Or the best roots and stems of meadow and lawn grasses may be chosen. All these are grown under good conditions at the plant breeders' farms, so that they become still better plants.

Certain pasture and lawn grasses have very small flowers and very little pollen. When men want to make a new kind of grass, they plant the several grasses close together in a plot, so that they will brush against each other. Then, each will put its pollen into the flower cups of some of the others. The wind too will help by scattering the light pollen among the crowded grasses.

In these and other ways the plant breeders have developed grasses that bear better grain for flour, and better cattle feed, and cane with more sugary juice. They have developed the plants so that they resist disease better, and will grow in hotter or colder parts of the world than the regions where they were first grown. They have made pasture grasses that can stand dry weather better, lawn grasses that grow in the shade as well as in the sun, and so on.

Today the seeds or plants of about fifty different pasture grasses can be bought from dealers. The farmer also has a choice of many varieties of corn, wheat and rice. He chooses the kind that is best for his particular purpose and will thrive best in the part of the country where his farm lies.

Whatever kinds of cultivated grasses he wants to grow, the seeds or plants the farmer buys are very different from the way they were fifty, a hundred, a thousand years ago.

Grass That Is Timber

The tallest grass in the world is bamboo. Its stems are hollow, but very strong. Some kinds are as much as seventy feet high and have stems over a foot thick. But there are other varieties that are ten to thirty feet tall, and a few that never grow more than a few inches. Most bamboos are found in warm or hot climates. But the tallest kinds, which grow only in the Far East, like places where the winters are cold and there is snow on the ground part of the year. They grow in Japan and China and some of the other Eastern countries.

The people split the thick stems and use them as
lumber to build their houses. Other bamboos of just

the right height and thickness are used as masts for sailboats. Bamboos from three to four inches thick are used as water pipes. For this the people have to bore through the joints, which are the only parts of the stem that are not hollow.

The lighter kinds of bamboos are used to make furniture, screens, umbrella frames, window shades, fishing poles, bird cages, baskets. And young, tender bamboo shoots are a favorite vegetable.

The men go to the bamboo forests and cut the tall, hard stems with strong, sharp knives or axes. The outer surface of bamboo is so hard that sparks fly when it is being chopped down.

When the bamboo falls the men trim off the leafy branches and load the stems on their carts or onto a truck. When they make building material out of the bamboo the planks have a rounded surface and are light brown. The outer surface is so hard and shiny that it sheds rain water well, and does not crack or wear off easily from heat, cold or storms. It is as good or better than paint.

Bamboo plants spread by putting out stemlike runners along the ground. These take root here and there, and the new shoots come up from them. The plants grow very fast—ten, twenty, sometimes even forty feet in a season. Some of the bamboo forests are so dense a man can hardly walk through them. Often men take cuttings from the stemlike runners of good, tall plants of a forest and plant them in other places to start new patches.

Other Grasses For Houses

Tall marsh and meadow grasses have long been used by primitive people to make their huts. Some of the people of Africa, South America, Australia and tropical islands still do.

Some Zulus of Africa, who live far from the white people's towns and cities, still make beehive-shaped grass houses. A number of these, set in a circle, make a little grass-house village called a kraal.

When a new hut is to be built, a spot is chosen for it. A father and son go up a creek, or along the banks of a lake. They look for tall reeds which are marsh and shore grasses. With sharp knives they cut them off close to the ground and strip them of their leafy tops, so that the reed stems are four to five feet long. They take handfuls of these and tie them into bundles.

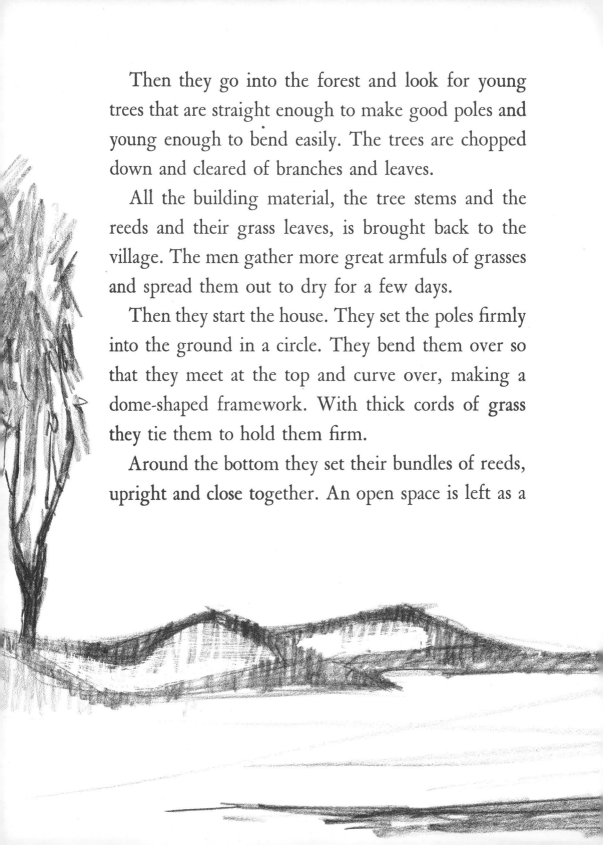

Then they go into the forest and look for young trees that are straight enough to make good poles and young enough to bend easily. The trees are chopped down and cleared of branches and leaves.

All the building material, the tree stems and the reeds and their grass leaves, is brought back to the village. The men gather more great armfuls of grasses and spread them out to dry for a few days.

Then they start the house. They set the poles firmly into the ground in a circle. They bend them over so that they meet at the top and curve over, making a dome-shaped framework. With thick cords of grass they tie them to hold them firm.

Around the bottom they set their bundles of reeds, upright and close together. An open space is left as a door. Next the men cover the upper part of the frame-work with the grass they gathered, making a thick thatch roof. Then their house is finished.

Grasses For Lawns

The grasses used for lawns in front of houses, on golf courses and in parks look different from any of the others. But they are just pasture grasses which are kept short by continual mowing. Because of this cutting the grasses never get a chance to grow coarse stems or seed heads, and so the lawns always feel and look like a soft green carpet.

Kentucky bluegrass, Bermuda, Manila, and several others make fine lawns on which to play games, or rest, or have picnics.

Grasses Protect the Land

Meadow grasses have wide-spreading roots that hold the soil. They keep the driving rain and the wind from sweeping it way. The slender grass blades form a thick tangle which shelters the earth, letting the rain water come through to the root more gently.

Beach grass, marsh grass, salt grass, sedge and rushes protect the shore lines of rivers, lakes and oceans. On the edge of the ocean the roots of the shore grasses keep the tides and waves from washing away too much of the sand and earth.

Rivers, brooks and creeks wash soil from unprotected banks and carry it to other places along their winding courses. Some of the soil drifts in among the roots and stems of shore grasses and settles there.

Grass builds up the land, too, for wherever it grows its old leaves and stems die and new grass springs up. The dead grass decays and becomes a part of the soil, enriching it.

In a swamp, or on the wet, shallow edge of a river or lake, the dead rushes, reeds or cord grasses, together with the soil that is washed in among them, gradually form new land that lies above the water. The new, soggy land dries out a little, and other plants begin to grow there—weeds, shrubs, or perhaps meadow grasses and some trees. Here, after hundreds of years, cattle will graze, or men will build factories and homes.

The grasses of the world are generous and bountiful. They not only provide people with many kinds of food, with furniture and houses, but they protect, enlarge and enrich the land they stand on.